ANDREW

TH

ANDREW LLOYD WEBBER
THE MUSICAL

MUSIC, LYRICS & BOOK BY
Nick Awde

DESERT ♥ HEARTS

First published in 2000
by Desert♥Hearts
PO Box 2131
London W1A 5SU
England

Reprinted May 2000, September 2000,
January 2001

© Nicholas Awde 1987, 1993, 2000

Typeset and designed by Desert♥Hearts

Printed and bound in Great Britain by
Cox & Wyman Ltd, Reading, England

British Library Cataloguing in Publication Data
A catalogue record for this book is available from the British Library

Library of Congress in Publication Data
A catalog record for this book has been requested

ISBN 1 898948 48 8

Music for the songs included in this volume is available as
'Andrew Lloyd Webber The Musical The Music'
(ISBN 1 898948 49 6)

Thanks to . . .

Nadia Cohen for being Nadia.
Lisa & John M. for post-production relief.
Jan Bourne for the first creative spark.
Andrew Honey & Pip Brennan for front-of-house spirit.
Marcela Diaz for being around.
Lou for comic relief.
Tom M. for general all-round talent.
Will Harvey, on whose lunch this was all based.
Paul & Kate Brennan, sorry I missed your wedding!
Jerry Berkowitz for remote-control support.
Jack Kroll for the phone calls.
Farouque Abdela for costumes in the original productions.
Sean, Ben & Nigel for endlessly bickering.
All those deserving, rising members of the theatrical profession
    who pitched in (and who prefer to remain unnamed)

            . . . and Mel Brooks, Zero Mostel & Gene Wilder
                        who gave us The Producers!

A brief note . . .

There were three major versions if not more of the original productions. The text here is the more or less original script – anyone interested in the popular 'cricket' version should contact the publishers. The musical was always planned to be a fluid entity and reflected the enormous number of changes in casts and productions that marked its development. It is intended to be flexible with respect to the insertion of subjects of topical humour as well as the modification of references that reflect the politics, life and times of the performance, performers and audience. Note, however, that each of the characters should have their own peculiar, distinctive accent and laugh, e.g. **Jesús** has a soft German accent (he is, incidentally, also heavily into leather). The eponymous hero of the show might wear a large coat with numerous internal pockets for shoving in whatever objects may come to hand as the show progresses. A streamlined cast would double up the character of **The Barman** with a pianist, placing a piano behind the bar, while the stage manager can always play **The Stage Manager**.

A Show for at Least Four Players

THE CAST

Part I:

The Leading Characters:

Andy Lloyb Webber	*Aspiring Composer of Musicals*
Tim Mandy-Rice Davies	*Aspiring Lyricist of Musicals*
Jesús	*Only Son of God*
The Barman	*Purveyor of Fine Spirits*

The Supporting Characters:

Ned's Atomic Sherry	*Impresario of the Stage*
David Frost-Springer	*Host of the TV Chat Show*
Cameron Dirty-Mac	*Impresario of the Stage*

The Extremely Essential but Not as Important Characters:

The Stage Manager	**An Actor**
The Warm-Up Man	**An Actress**
The Show Producer	**A Producer**
The Audition Hopefuls 1, 2, 3, 4 & 5	

*including George Formby,
Cliff Richard &
Elvis 'The King' Presley*

The Characters Who Dare Not Speak:

Julio Lluis Webber

Qué-Será-Será Bwightmán

Part II:

Jesús Perón
Judás Guevara
María Perón
MC Sally Bowles King Horríd
Pilates
A Critic of the Stage 1 & 2
A Reporter
A Director
A Producer

Suggested Doubling of Parts

Part I:

Andy Lloyb Webber:	A Producer
Tim Mandy-Rice-Davies:	An Actor
Jesús:	David Frost-Springer, An Actress
The Barman:	Ned's Atomic Sherry, Cameron Dirty-Mac, The Stage Manager, The Warm-Up Man, The Show Producer, The Audition Hopefuls 1, 2, 3, 4 & 5

Part II:

Jesús:	Jesús Perón
Tim:	Judás Guevara, A Critic of the Stage 1, A Director, Pilates
Andy:	María Perón, A Critic of the Stage 2, A Producer
Barman:	MC Sally Bowles King Horríd, A Reporter

ACT ONE

1. THE GLUMS

(**Andy** & **Tim** *are sitting in a pub, heads in hands, looking very glum indeed.*)

Andy & Tim (*Repeatedly sigh, look at each other as if to say something, change their minds, tut, look away into the distance.*)

Andy   (*Eventually.*) Hmm.

Tim   Um.

Andy   Hm.

Tim   Um. (*Nods head enthusiastically.*)

Andy   Mm mm. (*Grimaces and shakes head slightly.*)

(*They continue as before.*)

Andy & Tim You know . . . (*Laugh forcedly.*)

Andy   You first.

Tim   No, dear chap. I insist. (*Gestures.*)

Andy   No, Timmy, I absolutely insist.

Tim   No, Andy, I must absolutely insist.

Andy   No, Timmy, I do must absolutely insist!

Tim   Well if you insist. *(Sighs.)* I was only going to say that that song 'Don't Cry For Me'–

Andy   –'Clapham Junction'?

Tim   Hm. That's the one – 'Don't Cry for Me Clapham Junction'. Well, I was just going to say, Andy love, that it's a cracker. I've always thought that and I just want you to know.

Andy   Sweetie.

Tim   Thank you.

Andy   No. Have you got a sweetie?

Tim   Oh. Yes. Erm, no, I mean. *(Pulls pockets inside-out.)* Totally skint.

Andy   Well I suppose I'll have to have one of mine. *(Pulls out large box of chocolates.)*

Tim   And you?

Andy   You can have the orange ones.

Tim   No, I meant what did you did want to say before?

Andy   Well, I was just thinking the lyrics are jolly good for 'Don't Cry For Me Clapham Common'–

Tim   –'Junction'!

Andy   Bless you! They'll be humming it in the streets.

Tim   They were humming it long before we wrote it.

Andy   And it's the type of song that should bring the house down any day, in my book! *(Nods affirmatively at Tim, who nods back. They settle back into the above routine.)*

Andy   *(Suddenly.)* I mean, what's wrong with a musical called 'Ryvita'?

Tim   ' . . . The Story of a Grocer's Daughter Who Feels a Bit Sad After Winning the General Election' – nothing.

Andy   No! Nothing!

Tim   Exactly – 'Ryvita'–

Andy   ' . . . The Story of a Grocer's Daughter Who Feels a Bit Sad After Winning the General Election'. People just don't recognise quality.

Tim   Yes.

Andy   And they don't recognise me.

Tim   No.

Andy   Oh yes.

Tim   Yes!

Andy   No!

Tim   Mm!

(Silence.)

Andy   So why was that man so dreadfully unappreciative? What were the words he used . . . ? 'Boll . . .'

Tim   'Balls'?

Andy   No . . .

Tim   'Bollocks'!

Andy   Yes that was it. 'Bollocks'.

Tim   Mmm. But his dog liked it, I could tell!

Andy   Exactly!

Tim   He shouldn't have been there in any case – he thought it was Bingo night. I'm sure if there'd been anyone else in the audience, they would have loved it. Simply LOVED it!

Andy   Can't understand it. I just can't understand it–

Tim   It's just like our last musical–

Andy   'Beeching Express'–

Tim   –'The Story Of A Man Who Changed the Railways'.

Andy   Yes. 'Beeching Express'!

Tim   I thought it excellent that idea we had of running rails around the auditorium – bringing the smells and excitement of the railway to the appreciative audience.

Andy   Yes. Pity about the locomotives falling through the theatre floor.

Tim   Well it was difficult to get scale models . . . in any case, we thought real-life steam locomotives would be so much more–

Andy   Exciting.

Tim   Yes. Exciting . . . Pity about them falling through the floor.

Andy   Mm, and the fire.

Tim   Mm . . . and the criminal proceedings.

Andy   Well it wasn't our fault there were people sitting under the locomotive when it came crashing down.

Tim   Mm.

(Silence again. **Tim** *picks his nose, examines it, picks it again with great interest. He may choose to eat it.* **Andrew** *pats his hair prissily.* **Jesús** *enters, dressed in leather, boots, cap and moustache).*

Jesús   Hello!

Tim   Hey Zeus! My man! *(Lightens up and stands to greet his friend.)*

Jesús   Long time indeed. How've you been hanging?

Tim   Fine, just fine. Where've you been?

Jesús   Why, who's been talking? Who's the bit of fluff?

Tim   That's no fluff, that's my mate Andrew!

Jesús   Oh . . . aren't you going to introduce us?

Tim   Of course? Fluff – I mean, Andrew – Jesús, Jesús – Andrew.

Andy   *(Drawls.)* Oh hello.

Jesús   *(With interest.)* Hello!

Andy   *(Mouths silently to* **Tim**.*)* WHO IS HE?!

Tim   Jesús is an old friend of mine. He's a bit of a character really – been around quite a bit. His dad's got quite a bit of influence, let me tell you! *(Mouths to* **Andy**.*)* Jewish!

Andy   What? 'Swordfish'?

Tim   *(Out of the corner of his mouth, irritably.)* He's Jewish! *(Smiles and speaks normally.)* Bit of a dark horse.

Jesús   Now let's not start talking preferences, shall we, girls? *(Laughs.)* I do go back quite a way, though! And let's not just talk about me, shall we? Tell me all about your friend . . .

Andy   Well, funny you should mention it, I was just going.

Jesús	No you weren't, sit down.
Andy	Are you buying?
Jesús	Could be.
Andy	I might stay.
Jesús	Good. Barman, four glasses of water–
Tim	Four WHAT?
Jesús	For turning into wine! You were saying, Tim?
Tim	Well, this is the famous Andy I've been telling you about – he's a cool cat, you know. He writes all the music for my–
Andy	Our–
Tim	Our musicals.
Jesús	Do you really? Now there's a talented chappie.
Andy	*(Simpers with false modesty.)* Oh no, it's really nothing!
Jesús	So I've heard.
Andy	Pardon?
Jesús	*(Raises hand assuringly.)* Oh nothing. You know how cruel ignorant people can be.
Andy	Oh yes. I know.

Tim   Anyway, Jesús, we've just had another, dare I say it, flop on our hands. 'Ryvita'–

Jesús   '. . . The Story of a Grocer's Daughter Who Feels a Bit Sad After Winning the General Election'?

Andy   That's the one! Have you seen it?

Jesús   No, but I heard the dog quite enjoyed it.

Andy   Yes . . .

Tim   Anyway. We're at a bit of a crossroads really, we don't know where to go from here.

Andy   We've run out of ideas: 'Ryvita'–

Tim & Jesús   '. . . The Story of a Grocer's Daughter Who Feels a Bit Sad After Winning the General Election.'

Andy   –'Beeching Express', 'Strum and Prance' (my idea, that one!), 'Jonah and His Technicolor Yawn'–

Tim   'Whale'.

Andy   *(Wails.)*

Tim   No! The FISH! – 'Jonah and His Technicolor WHALE!'

Andy   'Whale' – we're at our wits' end!

Jesús   'Whale' I think I might have an idea . . .

2. A FORTUITOUS INTRODUCTION

(Lights dim and then come up again – **Andy**, **Tim** *&* **Jesús** *are now sitting around a table.)*

Jesús   So you see, I've had rather an interesting life, what with being the Only Son of God and all that. I've lived in the the Middle East. I'm a Jewish Christian. I've been crucified–

Tim   Haven't we all!

Jesús   –And risen from the dead. And my Second Coming–

Andy   Lucky if I can do it once!

Jesús   –Is still the subject of a great many news items all over the world. I'm still HOT and tropical!

Tim   –So you've kept a diary?

Jesús   You could say that.

Tim   Good, good, excellent. Yes I can see it now!

Andy   He's got it! Give the man room.

Tim   Yes, it's all becoming clear now. It has all the right elements, a tragedy of world proportions but with a silver lining! Young girl has God's Only Son. He grows up, deprived childhood in a lowly carpenter's home–

Jesús   Ugh, all those splinters!

Tim   –Against the odds to speak up for the poor and oppressed wherever they may be, spreading the word of peaceful revolution–

Andy   A kind of Gandhi meets Che Guevara.

Tim   That's it!

Andy   Yes! *(Snorts.)*

Tim   He makes friends – and enemies – falls in love with a fallen angel, his best friend betrays him, he's framed and gets a raw deal in court – justice is blind – and they take him off to–

Andy   The electric chair? *(Snorts.)*

Tim   –To be crucified with two lowly common criminals. But he has the last laugh – oh yes!–

Jesús   What?!

Tim   He rises from the dead and redeems Mankind!

Jesús   Of course! Brilliant!

Andy   Yes . . . !

Jesús   I'd never have believed that was MY life you've just pictured. Brilliant! When do you start writing?

Andy   Ah.

Tim   'Write'?

Andy   That means 'compose' too?

Jesús   Yes.

Andy   Ah.

Jesús   You're dispirited. I understand. From your previous failures.

Tim   Hm.

Jesús   Well haven't you got any new material you can use? Everyone's always got SOMETHING they're CURRENTLY working on!

Tim   Well, we have got one new song.

Andy   Yes. NO ONE'S heard it before. A sort of audible scoop, if you know what I mean! *(Chortles and snorts to himself.)*

Tim   It's very new!

Andy   It's very good.

Tim   It's WONDERFUL!

Andy   Marvellous! Just MARVELLOUS!

Tim   It's, it's, well it's a sort of audible revolution *(gesticulates as he strains to express the concept)* – it's real, it's pertinent, it's witty–

Andy   It'll touch you to the cockles of your heart.

Tim   It's just . . . so 'with it' and alive.

Andy   It's here.

Tim   It's NOW!

Jesús   Well, can we hear it then . . . ?

Andy & Tim   *(Look at each other.)*

Tim   Well it's not a hundred per cent finished–

Andy   No, you've got to imagine what it would be like if it were PROPERLY finished.

Tim   But we feel the structure's all there.

Andy   It obviously needs a little more polishing.

Tim   But I–

Andy   'We'!

Tim   –Think you'll get the idea.

Andy   *(To Tim.)* Shall we?

Tim   Shall we what?

Andy   You know *(nods seriously)* – DO it!

Tim   Oh ! Yes! Exactly. Sing you mean? It's called . . . um, we really haven't come up with a title yet.

Andy   Well, Tim, you know that's not quite true. We do in fact have a working title, *(beams at **Jesús**)* being the sort of professional chappies that we are.

Tim	'Tampons With Strings'.

Andy   We'll work on it.

Tim   It's *(grimaces as he reaches for the precise expression)* RELEVANT.

Andy   You'll see.

Tim   *(Still groping.)* It's–

Andy   Shall we?

Tim   Yes. Forgive the rusty voices. Uh one–

Andy   Uh two, ah!

Andy & Tim *(Clear throats.)*

Tim   Uh two.

TAMPONS WITH STRINGS
(Duet: **Andy** *&* **Tim***)*

Tim	**Fried onion bhajees**
Andy	**And fruit-flavoured undies**
Tim	**Old Holborn rollies**
Andy	**And strip poker parties . . .**
Tim	**Indian take-aways**
Tim & Andy	**Chinese and Thai**
Andy	**Such are some of my favorite items.***
Andy	**Athletic bodies**
Tim	**Tired hair with blonde highlights**
Andy	**Bedsits in Archway**
Tim	**And 'We don't fuck first nights'**

* The substitution here may be preferable of a better known line that rhymes with *'sings'.*

★

Andy	Healthfood and condoms
Tim & Andy	Aerobics and iMacs
Tim	Such are some of my favorite items.

Tim	Suntans from Elba
Andy	Clothes from Fiorucci
Tim	Après ski in swish San Moritz
Andy	Pediculture from Gucci

Tim	Habitat furniture
Tim & Andy	And Mothercare
Andy	Such are some of my favorite items.

Andy	Golf GTi's with
Tim	White leather upholstery
Andy	Brown speckled free-range eggs
Tim	From deep-litter poultry

Andy	Waitrose own fine brands
Tim & Andy	And tampons with strings
Tim	Such are some of my favorite items.

Tim	Covent Garden nightclubs
Andy	Tequila hangovers
Tim	Stocks, shares, index-linked interest
Andy	Plc take-overs
Tim	Filofax, quiches
T&A:	The FT share index
Andy	Such are some of my favorite items.

Tim	When the bomb drops
Andy	When my head aches
Tim	When it hurts to pee . . .
	I just recall
Tim & Andy	my favorite items . . .

**And consequently I don't feel . . .
So terrible at all!**

(Stunned silence.)

Andy   Well . . . what do you think?

Jesús   Er . . .

Andy   Oh! I just knew he wouldn't like it. I just KNEW it!

Jesús   No, no. I rather quite liked it.

Andy   He hated it! We should never, NEVER, reveal our songs until they're ready. I knew it wasn't ready, I just KNEW it! I told you Tim we shouldn't have done. I told you all along. What did I say?

Tim   Well it's your naff tunes.

Andy   I told you we should never . . . WHAT?!

Tim   I said: it's your naff tunes.

Andy   My naff tunes?!

Tim   Yeah, don't give up the day job. Though if you ask me, sexing chickens could hardly be described as a job, day or otherwise.

Andy   The 'day job'? Oooh! you said you wouldn't tell anyone! Let me tell YOU something, Mr So-Called Lyricist, if you put Wisden to words it would sound better than the offal you bring up that passes for 'lyrics'! *(Jabs* **Tim** *in the chest.)*

Tim   'The offal I bring up'? My lyrics? 'Offal'?
What about the PIG'S TESTICLES you call 'music'?
(Jabs **Andy** *in the chest.)*

Andy   'Pig's testicles'? 'Pig's testicles'? Well, what
about the dog's pizzle you present as words – *(Pushes* **Tim**
in the chest.)

Tim   'Dog's pizzle'? I'll give you 'dog's pizzle'!

*(***Tim*** pushes* **Andy** *over and follows him down for a brief and
extremely undignified scuffle.* **Tim** *ends up on top screaming,*
Andy *underneath, screeching.)*

Tim   Are you going to give up?

Andy   *(Wails and drums his feet heavily on the ground
in reply.)*

Jesús   Come on, come on girls. Stop it! You'll
never get anywhere like this! Can't anyone do anything?

Barman   I know . . . ! *(Throws bucket of water over
them.)* They always get like this.

Jesús   Oh no, we've baptised them! *(Waits until they
quieten down.)* Well, what a scene. What a to-do! Not a
particularly impressive pair are you? Some partnership . . . !
When are you ever going to get your shits together?

Tim   HE'S the shit!

Andy   ME?! *(Scuffle starts afresh.)* I'll see you in court!

Tim   Handbags at dawn!

(Jesús and The Barman are reduced to hauling them away from each other. They continue to hold them, half off the floor, snapping and snarling at each other.)

Andy   Listen matey! One day I'll be SO famous NO ONE'll be able to ever treat me the way you do!

Tim   Aren't you confusing 'being famous' with 'taking other people's credit'?!

Andy   *(Fishgulps. They lunge again.)*

Jesús   I think it's time to face up to the fact that you've BOTH got a problem. I mean, after all, one can only take SO much recycled canned Puccini!

*(Both **Andy** and **Tim** suddenly stop snarling – as if they have been doused with water again. They look at each other, at **Jesús**, back at each other.)*

Andy   But, but– *(Continues 'but-ing'.)*

Jesús   No, no, hold on, let me finish. Well, Puccini isn't quite enough, is he?

Andy   But, but, but Puccini's pop music!

Jesús   Yes – but he's been dead for a century!

Tim   But so's Buddy Holly.

Andy   Who?

*(**Jesús** & **Tim** look at **Andy** speechless.)*

Jesús   I think you might just have touched on the problem. Your music's not relevant. It's not hip!

Andy   Benjamin Britten. He's jolly good.

Jesús   No, that's NOT what I mean! Something's got to be done about the music!

Tim   Heh, heh!

Jesús   Ah, but the writing sucks too!

Tim   Ah–

Andy   Heh, heh, heh!

Tim   What's the matter with my writing?

Andy   You can't do joined up yet!

(**Jesús** & **Tim** *both turn and stare at* **Andy**. *Look at each other, sigh, then carry on from where they left off.*)

Jesús   Your dialogue's fine – don't get me wrong! And so are your lyrics – well . . . Potiphar's wife singing to Jonah: 'Hey, hey baby/Why don't you come over here/And fuck me till I fart!' is perhaps a little on the, um, blunt side.

Tim   I thought it had a certain poetry. No one's complained.

Jesús   Well, yes you could say that – well that's not the point! The point is that your dialogues and lyrics are all rather hampered – CASTRATED let's say – by the storylines.

Tim   Really?! For example?

Jesús   For example, a very good example, 'Jonah and his Technicolor Whale'?!

Tim   Yes?

Jesús   Where's the hook in that?

Tim   He doesn't catch the whale – it catches him – it doesn't use a hook.

Jesús   I didn't mean that. Where's the message?

Tim   Um.

Jesús   Where's the . . . art? Do you see what I mean?

Tim   Well it was VERY hard to find a lead player.

Andy   Yes. YOU try and find a whale right for the part!

Tim   And one with an Equity card!

Barman   'Scuse me!

Everyone Else Yeah WHAT?

Barman   That doesn't matter any more.

(Everyone else stops momentarily. They look at him. Ignore him. Carry on as normal.)

Andy   Yeah, YOU try. At the auditions most of them were too cut up and just blubbered on the stage!

Jesús   . . . And why was Jonah always in cricket gear?

Tim   Well . . . They used to wear that sort of thing, didn't they?

Jesús   IT WAS A <u>BIBLICAL</u> STORY FOR CHRIST'S–

Andy   Tut, tut. *(Raises finger.)*

Jesús   FOR <u>MY</u> SAKE! No one wore cricket gear in the Old Testament.

Tim   What? Not even the umpires?

Jesús   Nein.

Tim   You KNOW you can't get higher than a six in cricket. What about the New Testament?

Jesús   No! Not even in the New Testament! The game of cricket was not even invented then . . . !

Andy & Tim *(Silence. Look at each other.)*

Tim   Well, I suppose they didn't have counties in those days.

Jesús   But look! You've got Jonah, and you've got a Whale, and you've got a classic tale from the Bible. How does cricket fit in?

Andy & Tim *(Silence. Look at each other.)*

Tim   *(Lamely.)* It . . . it was essential to the plot.

Andy   Yes, essential.

Tim   Shut up!

Andy   I was only helping.

Tim   You only write the music. *(To* **Jesús**.*)* But it was essential.

Jesús   Essential? In fact, and do correct me if I am wrong, but am I right in suggesting that cricket crops up quite frequently in your musicals?

Tim   Um.

Andy   Um.

Tim   Yes.

Andy   Yes.

Jesús   In fact, would I be right in thinking that cricket crops up in every one of your musicals?

Tim   Well . . . *(Shifts from one foot to the other and thinks hard. Starts to say something. Doesn't. Repeats this. Speaks finally.)* Yes.

Jesús   In fact, every single thing you've ever done degenerates into a cricket commentary – even the love scenes?

Tim   Um. *(Nods wrily.)*

(Silence. **Andy** *&* **Tim** *suddenly brighten up.)*

Tim   You see it was essential for the plot–

Andy   –Essential for the plot, yes!–

Tim   –in 'Jonah and the Amazing Technicolor Whale'. Everyone wants Jonah's nice shiny-white cricket gear, and they'll stop at nothing to get it. Yes. It happened to me at school – everyone wanted my box. No, they did! You see it's all based on real human experience, the human touch of authenticity. This is 'where it's at' theatre. Cricket is a metaphor of life. Yes! *(Makes a fist to emphasise his point.)* The detail of a match is a veritable microcosm of the Great Game that is Life. *(Grows louder, punching the air.)* A Test Series, the struggle between the forces of good and evil, Light and Darkness – *(The others look at each other in desperation.)* – THE ASHES ARE THE SYMBOL OF THAT GREAT GOAL, THAT GREAT END TOWARDS WHICH WE ALL STRIVE, YES!! THE ASHES ARE THE SYMBOL OF THAT DESTINATION OF ALL MANKIND, OUR DESTINY, OUR . . . <u>DEATH</u>! *(Looks expectantly around at the others. Awkward silence.)*

Jesús   All I said was your writing was a bit naff.

(Pause.)

Andy   So what you're saying is we need a good story?

Jesús   Yes.

Tim   Well, your life story seems as good as any.

Jesús   Well I'm all for it – it certainly needs an update, and we could make a packet from the movie rights!

Andy   And if 'Marie Claire' serialised it!

Tim   And the sequel.

Jesús   But you've got to get your shits together–

Andy & Tim What?!

Jesús   Look. Let's play a game.

Andy & Tim Oh no, not a game!

Jesús   No it's not what you think. Trust me. This is a little something I used to do before curing the blind, raising the dead, you know that sort of thing. *(Pats **Andy** on the arse.)* This'll relax you and get the creative juices flowing–

Andy   *(Aside.)* And that's not all by the look in his trousers.

Jesús   –It's something I've used lots of times–

Andy   *(Aside.)* I really don't doubt it!

Jesús   –So what I'm going to do is to give you Tim some words, purely at random, and I want you to simply say whatever comes first to mind.

Tim   Whatever?

Jesús   Whatever. All right. Ready?

Tim   Yep! *(Rolls up sleeves.)*

Jesús   Umm, let me see . . . What would you reply if I said to you, 'Musical'?

Tim   Cricket.

Jesús   Okay. Let's try another word, um, let me see,
'Lyrics'?

Tim   *(Slight pause.)* Cricket.

Jesús   Fine. Um, 'Opera'?

Tim   Cricket.

Jesús   *(Without irony.)* Yes, yes, I can see, this is
getting us somewhere. We'll change tack now, 'Whale'?

Tim   Cricket.

Jesús   'Steam engine'?

Tim   Cricket.

Jesús   'Love'?

Tim   Cricket.

Jesús   'Squishy bits'?

Tim   *(Thinks.)* Yep, cricket!

Jesús   *(Thinks.)* 'Sex'?

Tim   *(Thinks a bit more.)* Cricket!

Jesús   Oh this is preposterous! You can't possibly
associate sex with cricket!

Tim   Second Test in Australia, 1963 – pure orgasm!

Andy   What about me?

Jesús & Tim   What about you?!

Andy   Well, the music. I write the music. Go on, play the game with me.

Tim   *(Smiles at* **Jesús***.)* Excuse me. *(Turns, hooks arm around* **Andy***'s neck, jabs him violently in the eye.)* You were saying?

Jesús   Maybe we SHOULD try it on him – if at the very least to shut him up.

Andy   Oh yes!

Jesús   *(Sighs.)* I know we're going to regret this . . . 'Music'.

Andy   Puccini.

Jesús   'Opera'.

Andy   Puccini.

Jesús   'Musical'?

Andy   Puccini.

Jesús   'Puccini'?

Andy   *(Silence.)* . . . Puccini.

Jesús   'Rock'n'roll'.

Andy   Ah . . . Puc– what?!

Jesús   Aha! 'What?!' Yes, this is very interesting. Yes, yes, here you see the problem we have here.

Tim   What?

Jesús   Exactly – 'what' is the question indeed. I think our young Andrew here doesn't know the meaning of 'rock'n'roll'.

All   *(Dramatic intake of breath.)*

Jesús   Yes. I'm afraid it's that bad.

Tim   So what's your diagnosis?

Jesús   Not good. You're going to have to learn to live with it.

Andy   I could learn!

Jesús   What, to live with it?

Andy   No – This rock'n'roll thingy.

Tim   He's right – he could learn rock'n'roll . . . couldn't he?

Jesús   Um

Tim   Please!

Jesús   No.

Andy   Go on, give us a try!

Jesús   Well you can't just do something like that

overnight. Mmm, but do bear in mind that you need
rock'n'roll – in fact the WHOLE world needs rock'n'roll
right now. Puccini is not enough–

All (*Dramatic intake of breath.*)

Jesús –Yes, yes! I'm sorry you had to hear it this
way, but Puccini is simply not enough for the modern
world! We need operas now with pzazz, a message, a big
juicy promo record and . . .

Tim Rock'n'roll!

Andy So let me try!

Jesús Very well. Repeat after me: 'De Dop A Moola
. . .'*

Andy 'Be Bop A WHAT?!'

Jesús Go on. don't analyse – just have a bash –
you'll get the hang of it. Now after me: 'De Dop A Moola.'

Andy 'De'– sorry, sorry– no, don't help me, I'll get
it . . . 'DE Dop A Moola.'

Jesús 'She's my laydee.'

Andy 'She's my layDEE.'

Jesús 'De Dop A Moola.'

Andy 'De Dop A Moola.'

Jesús 'I don't mean perhaps.'

* One is encouraged to substitute here a more commonly known sequence of the time, such as
'Be Bop A Lula', 'Ram A Lam A Ding Dong' or possibly even 'Awopbopaloobopawopbamboom'.

Andy   'I don't mean perhaps.'

Jesús   Now put it all together.

Andy   All together? Oof!

Jesús   Take your time.

Tim & Barman Yeah, take your time Andy!

(Jesús, Tim & The Barman urge Andy on.)

Andy   Well, here goes! Jolly difficult – 'De Dop A Moola/ She's my laydee/De Dop A Moola/I don't mean perhaps'! Yes!

(Entire cast erupts with joy.)

Andy   I've got it!

Jesús   He's got it!

Andy   I've got it!

Tim & Jesús He's got it!

Andy   I've got it!

Jesús, Tim & Barman He's got it!

Andy   'The rain in Cleethorpes' . . . 'España'? – No! 'The rain in Rochdale' . . . No, no, oh, I feel like I could fly! Oh, I've got a little song! In a plane! Oh! I've got a little song!

Jesús, Tim & Barman He's got a song, he's got a little song!

Andy   I've got a little song! And it's just a little bit rock and roll! *(Wiggles leg and sings song again.)*

All   Hooray!

*(**Andy** and cast frolic happily about stage singing 'De Dop A Moola' etc. – with **Andy** placing different stress on each word every time he sings a fresh phrase ('De DOP A Moola/She's my layDEE!!', 'DE Dop A MOOla/She's MY laydee' and so on) until finally . . .)*

Jesús   *(Stops and waves arms about. Everyone stops except for **Andy** who carries on blithely unaware.)* Stop! Stop, everyone! It's no good. Let's face it, it's still not going to work!

*(Suddenly **Andy** and **Tim** seem to slump. They look crestfallen).*

Andy   But I'm a genius! Aren't I, Trevor?

Tim   Tim.

Andy   Tim. So we'll move to Nashville.

Tim   And write country and western advertising jingles! Yes!

Andy   'Don't Cry for Me Ryvita'.

Tim   'Don't Cry for Me Ribena'

Andy   You'll see – they'll be sorry!

Jesús   No, there's no need for drama.

Tim   Oh, so we can put cricket in?

Jesús   No! There's no need to lose hope. What have we got?

Tim   Not a lot!

Andy   I'm still a genius, though.

Jesús   No. You've got my story and your words and music – there's the germ of something BIG here – all it needs is a little application. A little mental Vaseline!

Andy   *(Scribbles.)* 'Germans and Vaseline.'

Jesús   Yes. Rock'n'roll and the life of Christ – MOI!

Andy   Eh? That'll never work! *(Scribbles down the idea.)*

Tim   Yes!! Of course. Christ does a heist. Religious boss on a cross. Elvis was Jesús! I can see it now!

Andy   Tut. But those rhinestone suits would be RUINED in the crucifixion scenes.

Jesús   No. The life of Jesús Christ, in an opera set to rock music. Got it?

Tim   Like a vision. Elvis!

Andy   How do you spell 'Denzil'?

Jesús   NO – Elvis! MOI!

Andy   We could do great things, Jesús!

Jesús   It's almost written! Now all you need is a cast! So what are you waiting for?

Tim   Waiting – CREATING.

Andy   Right on, Don.

Tim   Tim.

Andy   Thank Jesús– *(Looks up slyly.)* Ah. *(Raises finger and winks.)* Thank YOU!

(Andy *&* **Tim** *march off to a pub table in order to write their musical).*

Ned   *(Rises from his seat.)* Pardon moi!

Tim   Yes?

Andy   Who are you!

Ned   Nedine's Atomic Sherry's the name, and I couldn't help overhearing your conversation. I'm a great admirer of youthful vigour, a GREAT admirer *(looks meaningfully at* **Andy***)* and I'm a theatrical producer of the theatre. If you can come up with a cracker of a rock opera, I'll give you a shot in the West End!

Andy & Tim   Oh jolly good!

(Andy & *Tim scamper away to write musical.)*

Jesús   That's very kind of you, Mr, er?

Ned   Sherry, Ned Sherry, but just call me 'Atomic' why don't you?

Jesús   All right *(smiles and pauses slightly)* – 'Atomic'. That was very kind of you. I hope they don't disappoint you.

Ned   *(Laughs.)* Well we'll see. Am I right in assuming that it's your life story they're basing it on?

Jesús   That's correct.

Ned   So what've you been doing with yourself since the . . . um? *(Gesticulates vaguely as* **Jesús** *watches slightly bemused.)*

Jesús   Nothing much. Wandered around the world for a couple of thousand years. You know how it is. And then finally decided to settle down. Got a nice flat in Chingford, nice job in the City, good perks.

Ned   You're a banker?

Jesús   *(Looks quizzically with a half-smile at the audience – starts to say something. Stops. Changes his mind. Beams at the audience.)* No, a chartered accountant.

Ned   But you look remarkably healthy. I mean I know things can heal quite well over two thousand years, but didn't they, you know, didn't they, um, well you know? *(Jabs palms of hands.)*

Jesús   Didn't they what?

Ned   Well, you know – it's just that you look a bit, well, ALIVE to me! You catch my meaning?

Jesús   Of course I'm alive – there's no point in going on BUPA if you're not ALIVE!

Ned   But didn't they, you know, CRUCIFY you?

Jesús   Oh yes! But I rose from the DEAD afterwards!

Ned   Didn't it hurt?

Jesús   No, I just ROSE, and there I was, rising, with all these disciples saying, 'Lo and behold, He is risen!' You know, one moment going down, and the next – rising! A bit frustrating, but no pain–

Ned   No, I mean DYING – did it hurt when they, you know.

Jesús   Oh! You mean CRUCIFIXION!

Ned   Yes.

Jesús   No. But all that hanging round . . . !

Ned   Hm. All this talk of rising, honestly, it's making me quite flustered. Ah, one last thing before I part. Tell me – oh no I can't possibly!

Jesús   No go on. You've thought it, and you know what they say about 'word, thought and deed'!

Ned   Oh, no, it's too personal. You'll think I'm prying.

Jesús   No, go on!

Ned   Well, it's always intrigued me. You see, whenever I feel myself in the heat of the moment achieving a sexual climax I cry out 'Oh Jesús!' – if you're Jesús, what do you cry out when you come?

Jesús   Well why don't we find out?

(They walk out arm in arm. **Ned's Atomic Sherry** *can be just heard saying as they go out the door: "You know, I've had a few deities in my time, but never a trinity!" or "Three into one goes more easily than you think!")*

3. A FINE COMPANY

(The next morning. Cast in pub looking gloomy.)

Andy & Tim *(Burst through pub door looking very, very happy.)* We've done it!

Jesús Done what?

Andy We've got a script worked out – it's a cracker!

Tim And the music's not bad either!

Jesús Hang on, hang on. Honestly! Quiet please, less hysteria! *(Silence as he views them quizzically.)*

Andy Well a peculiar thing happened, Tim was flipping – weren't you Tim?

Tim Oh yes Andy I was. Flipping–

Andy –Through the Bible (such a jolly book – I never realised how simply DRAMATIC religion could be!) and I–

Tim –We–

Andy *(Stops. Looks hard and long at **Tim**.)* I suddenly had this idea–

Tim *(Coughs.)* Yes. So we've ditched your life story–

Jesús   What?!

Tim   Well, luvvy, SOME of the details.

Andy   For the time being, of course. We might come back to it.

Tim   Per se.

Andy   We might keep the dying bit in.

Tim   Yes, but we've just got to get all that violence sorted out – after all, no one gets crucified in 'The Sound of Music', do they?

Jesús   No, but the audience does.

Andy   Ah. Well . . .

Jesús   So what about the musical?

Tim   Sorry. You see, we got this idea–

Andy   –In a blinding flash–

Tim   That's the one!

Andy   –And realised that there were other sides to Jesús's life that were just so sweet and tender–

Tim   A sort of 'Romeo and Juliet' meets 'Silence of the Lambs'–

Andy   And all those mangers!

Tim   –That we just had to do it!

Andy   Yes!

Tim   So obvious really, we don't even know how we missed it in the first place!

Andy   But–

Tim   Rather than start all over again–

Andy   Indeed, rather than start all over again–

Tim-   We decided to recycle–

Andy   So to speak –

Tim   –Our last almost-made-it hit–

Andy   'Jonah And His Amazing Technicolor Yawn'–

Tim   –'Whale'–

Andy   *(Wails.)* 'Jonah And His Amazing Technicolor Whale' –

Tim   And rename it–

Andy   'Jesús And His Amazing Technicolor Whale.' *(Wails.)*

Tim   It's a winner!

Andy   It's a hit!

Jesús   *(Stunned silence.)*

Tim   And we even put in some of our own
experiences.

Andy   Yes. We've suffered too.

Tim   Yes. The personal touch–

Andy   –Of authenticity.

Jesús   *(Stunned silence.)*

Tim   Some of our reminiscences.

Andy   Yes.

Jesús   *(Stunned silence.)*

Tim   You see, we found out that the bittersweet
trials–

Andy   –And tribulations–

Tim   –Of Jesús's early life–

Andy   –Of YOUR early life–

Tim   –Were exactly–

Andy   Uncannily–

Tim   –Eerily like our own experiences–

Andy   So–

Tim   –We've kind of . . . mixed . . . them up . . . !
(Looks quizzically at **Jesús**.*)*

Andy   –Together . . .

Jesús   *(Starts to fume and shake.)*

Tim   And not too too much cricket . . .

Jesús   *(Explodes wordlessly and stamps about helplessly.)*

Tim   We could always write out the part of the
whale!

Jesús   *(Continues to explode wordlessly and stamp about
helplessly.)*

Andy   See. I told you he'd like it . . .

Tim   *(Thinks.)* I'll get an Oscar for this. 'Jesús and
His Amazing Technicolor Whale'!

Andy   *(Wails.)* Oh yes.

Tim   Yes!

Andy   *(Starts to say 'yes', changes his mind.)* No!

Tim   What?!

Andy   No, Timmy dear, I do believe we need a better
title . . . ! We'll call it 'Jesús-María Christ Super-Estar'!

Jesús   *(Drily.)* Gives it just the Mediterranean
flavour it needed, I suppose!

Tim   Exactly! Now we need a cast.

Andy   Yes, a 'cast'! *(They start to scamper out again.)*

Jesús   Hang on girls.

Andy & Tim What?

Tim   We've got a cast to find.

Jesús   Well, don't you need a director?

Andy   A what?

Jesús   A director. Someone who directs. Every show needs to be directed. This means you need a director.

Andy & Tim Oh.

Jesús   If it's my life story I'd like a bit more involvement – hands on – it's a bit sacred to me, you understand, especially since it affects members of my family. *(Smiles sweetly.)* Or perhaps you already have a director?

Tim   No – I mean, yes . . . We HAVE already got a director.

Andy   You see, we've always used the same director–

Tim   –Being the type of professionals–

Andy   –That we are.

Jesús   So where is he?

Tim   Who?

Jesús   Your director.

Andy & Tim Ah . . . *(Look at each other.)*

Jesús   I mean, is he going to like the idea? Has he
even seen the script? What ideas does he have for the
lead? (I rather fancy someone in the Gielgud mould to
play the part of me.) A rock and roll opera is a bit new-
fangled, isn't it?

Tim   Hmm.

Andy   He's a bit classically-minded.

Tim   You see, we've never had the intention of
falling prey to nepotism.

Andy   And we'd never want to be accused of
favouritism

Tim   But it's his brother–

Andy   Julio–

Tim   His flesh and blood–

Andy   The cellist–

Tim   But he can direct in his sleep!

Andy   Yes. He sleeps all the time.

Tim   He's only a cellist when he's thinking!

Jesús   So where is he, this brother of yours?

Andy   (*Indicates with a nervous flick of his head the table where* **Julio Lluis Webber** *and* **Qué-Será-Será Bwightmán** *are seated.*)

Jesús   Where?

Andy   (*Repeats head flick.*) You know!

Jesús   I don't know.

Andy   Him!

Jesús   Who . . . Oh, not the . . .

Tim   Yes. You don't have to say it . . .

Jesús   The person sitting over there with the floozy?

Andy   'Floozy'? 'FLOOZY'? That happens to be my wife! How dare you!

Tim   Yes.

Jesús   But he's a blow-up doll!

Andy   No, it's not – it's my brother.

Jesús   But he's a blow-up doll. SHE'S a blow-up doll!

Andy   It runs in the family. How dare you insult us. Julio takes after my grandmother. And if he weren't feeling a bit light-headed today, I'm sure he'd show you a thing or two! Hmph!

Tim *(Touches **Andy**'s arm reassuringly.)* Oh, it doesn't matter, Andy – go on!

Andy Oh all right. Honestly, the things we artists have to put up with! Julio?

Julio *(**Andy** provides the voice of **Julio**, squeaked badly from the side of his mouth.)* Yes?!

Andy Would you like to step over here for a moment, dear?

Julio Oh, all right.

*(**Andy** walks over and carries **Julio** over – **Julio** farts, **Andy** says in apologetic aside to audience: 'Wind!'.)*

Jesús He's a blow-up doll – you made him move!

Andy I didn't.

Tim Okay, he may not be human – or even alive – but he's the best we've got.

Andy The best we can afford.

Tim He's a great choreographer! Best Dance of the Seven Veils this side of Catford!

Andy And my brother! What greater recommendation?

Tim Julio – do you think our rock and roll opera is a good idea?

Julio	Yes!
Jesús	YOU just said that.
Andy	I didn't.
Jesús	You did, I saw you!
Andy	No. He's just got a bit of a cold!
Tim	And he's shy.
Jesús	Julio do you think it'll work?
Julio	Yes!
Andy	What? *(Listens.)* Oh and he says it'll be a smash!
Jesús	He said no such thing! That's a blow-up dolly. Blow-up dollies can't talk!
Tim	Ah now you've hurt his feelings.
Jesús	Ah.
Andy	I'd apologise if I were you.
Jesús	What?!
Tim	Apologise.
Andy	*(Hisses quietly.)* Otherwise he might not want to direct – you know how highly strung geniuses can be!
Jesús	*(Defiant silence.)*

Tim   Well?

Jesús   Well what?

Tim   *(Explains with a cough, gesture and raised eyebrows.)*

Jesús   No . . . ! Oh very well. Julio, even if you are only a blow-up dolly, I apologize. *(**Julio** moves.)* What's that?

Andy   *(To **Julio**.)* Pardon? . . . Oh yes.

Jesús   What did he say?

Andy   Julio's just said – you know, it's his cold – he accepts your apology, and he understands your initial antagonism. And he says he might direct the opera!

Andy, Tim & Barman   Hooray! *(Kiss and hug **Julio**.)*

Andy   Ah, ah. If you say 'please'.

Jesús, Tim & Barman   What?

Andy   *(To **Julio**.)* What's that? Ah, if you say PRETTY please.

Jesús   If I–? No.

Andy   Ooh, I think you'd better.

Tim   Go on.

Jesús   I will not say 'pretty please' or 'please' of any type to an assortment of gaseous rubber genitals!

Andy & Tim Oh go on . . . The show . . .

Jesús No!

Andy & Tim Please!

Jesús Oh okay . . . Julio, will you direct our opera, please–

Andy Ah, ah!

Jesús PRETTY please!

Andy *(Listens.)* Julio says thank you and yes he will direct our rock and roll opera.

Jesús Well thank you Jul- *(Explodes.)* God I can't believe I've just apologised to a rubber fuck . . . ! *(Puts head in hands.)*

Tim Ah don't worry Jesús, he'll do a really good job, you wait and see–

Andy –After all, he's a genius!

Jesús Okay, okay, so now we've got a director. Now we need–

Tim A cast?

Jesús A cast.

4. CASTING NOT DROWNING

(Sign on door says: 'TONITE AUDTIONS – ALL WELKOM!')

Jesús   Who's first?

Barman   Female lead – the part of Mary Magdalene.

Jesús   Oh yes of course.

Barman   *(Calls out.)* Yes please! *(Enter* **Qué-Será-Será Bwightman***, blow-up doll – sits there in silence.)* Qué-Será-Será Bwightman, actress and (ahem) singer . . .

Andy   Yes wonderful! Marvellous!

Tim   We've got a star on our hands!

Andy   What a performance!

Jesús   *(Sighs quietly.)* Next!

Barman   Male lead – the part of Jesús.

Tim   We need a star

Andy   No, better, we need a rock and roll star – after all, this is a rock and roll opera!

Tim   A REAL star!

Andy   Yes – Walt Whitman!

Barman   Is he a composer?

Andy   Yehudi Menuhin!

Tim   'Scuse me. *(Turns and knees **Andy** in groin.)*

Barman   Elvis?

Andy   *(Squawks.)* Yes, Elvis!

Jesús   *(Sarcastically.)* And the Rolling Stones could understudy.

Julio   Mmm mm.

Jesús   What was that?

Tim   Ah, Julio says he thinks an unknown might be a good idea.

Jesús   All right, we won't get Elvis.

Andy   Anyway, you can never get him off the toilet. He's such a strain . . .

Jesús   Call the first!

1st Hopeful   *(George Formby singing 'My Way'.)*

Jesús   We'll have less of that jazz thank you! – Next!

2nd Hopeful   *(Heavy metal screecher.)*

Jesús   Nice trousers. Next!

3rd Hopeful *(A bearded Christ in Nazi SS uniform.)*

Jesús *(Before 3rd Hopeful can sing a word.)* Next!

4th Hopeful *(Elvis Presley.)*

Jesús Too Elvis – we need more . . . Cliff Richard. *(Before he can sing a word – a Cliff Richard cutout pops up.)* No, you shouldn't take the word of God too literally!

5th Hopeful *(Jason Donovan.)*

Jesús Too . . .

(All vomit.)

Barman *(After the last hopeful has left.)* So what are we going to do now?

(Everyone looks very glum.)

Andy Well we could always karaoke it, couldn't we?

(Even glummer silence . . .)

Jesús Oh all right. I'll do it – no no, you don't have to twist my arm. And no – don't try to stop me. I'll make the sacrifice – for the Fatherland – I cannot disappoint my public. No, I must insist you don't try to stop me. Yes! I'll play the part of Jesús!

(Everyone looks at him blankly and a trite incredulously.)

Tim *(Suddenly.)* Oh all right.

Andy   Next!

Jesús   What's the next part?

Barman   The part of Judás.

Andy   Ooh no, that'll never do – all that betrayal and suicide. There's no tragedy! He'll have to go!

Tim   Hm, but he does get to wear nice shiny cricket togs . . .

Andy   Judás in nice shiny cricket togs?

Jesús   Judás? Cricket?! Oh no!

Andy   You never told us.

Tim   Well, I was keeping it as a sort of suprise.

Andy   Jolly good. You can play Judás then!

Tim   I was hoping you'd say that. Next?

Barman   The part of King Horríd.

Andy   Ah, now . . . no.

Tim   No, no.

Andy   Hmmm.

Tim   Hmm.

Andy   *(Sharp intake of breath. Shakes head.)* No.

Tim   He'll just have to go.

Andy   But, but, I wrote a nice song for him!

Tim   Oh all right. Horríd's in. The Barman can do him.

Jesús   So . . . that leaves us with . . .?

Barman   Assorted apostles, disciples, townsfolk and general hangers-on.

Jesús   That's all?

Barman   Oh no, I forgot the poor and needy.

Tim   Hmm.

Barman   And the diseased and generally crippled.

Tim   Oh no.

Andy   No, no.

Tim   Not really.

Andy   You see, we always like to present good wholesome FAMILY entertainment.

Tim   It's the name of our game!

Barman   Well that's not very equal opportunities of you, is it? Giggle!

(Tense silence, the others glare at **The Barman**.*)*

Andy   *(Simply, suddenly and matter-of-factly.)* We
employed Prince Edward.

Tim   We'll have to use the audience–

Andy   Audience participation! *(Leers at audience and
smiles cheekily.)*

Tim   –For the rest of the cast. AND they've
already paid.

Andy   But far be it from us to suggest that we USE
people!

Tim   Far be it!

Andy   But I'm sure they all know how a chorus-line
goes.

Tim   They'll pick up the lines.

Barman   Audience interaction, I like it!

Tim   –The foreskin of theatre, oh yes! I think
you'll find that we're well known for that sort of thing!

Jesús   Good.

Andy   That's that settled!

Barman   Not quite. No show is complete without the,
um . . .

Andy, Tim & Jesús   Yes?

Barman   You know, the . . .

Andy, Tim & Jesús   The WHAT?

Stage Manager   *(Offstage.)* The producer!

(Ned's Atomic McSherry *bounds on to the stage and acts in a producerly manner.)*

       THE PRODUCER'S SONG
       (**Actress, Actor, Producer, Barman,**
       Stage Manager *&* **Ensemble**)

Ensemble   Producer of the show
       He's producer of the show
       You've all gotta go
       'Cos he's producer of the show
Actress   So see me dance
       And see me prance
       He's gonna make me a big star!

Ensemble   Producer of the show
       He's producer of the show
       You've all gotta go
       'Cos he's producer of the show

Actor   So hear me roar
       Hear them scream for more
       He's gonna make me a big star!

Actress   I could play the female lead
       I've trained you see
       To be a star on the stage
       To take my share of fame
       I'm not afraid of casting couches
       It's plain to see – So let's give it a try!

★

	So where's the part?
Ensemble	(Could she wear a pop-on glitter ball?)
Actress	So where's the part?
Ensemble	(She'll take a part no matter how small!)
Actress	Which role am I going to play?
Ensemble	(She'll join the chorus just like before!)
Actress	I can sing and dance so whaddya say?

Actor	I'd be so good for the male lead role
	Oh can't you see?
	I'm so cool and bland
	Why don't you come take me in hand?
	And even though my vocal range won't hit high C
	Come on give me a try!

	So where's the part?
Ensemble	(Could he wear a hard cricket box?)
Actor	So where's the part?
Ensemble	(Would he look good in shiny white cricket togs?)
Actor	Which role am I going to play?
Ensemble	(He'll join the chorus just like before!)
Actor	I can sing and dance, so whaddya say?

Ensemble	Producer of the show
	He's producer of the show
	You've all gotta go
	'Cos he's producer of the show

Producer	I'm the producer of the show tonight
	But it's sad you see
	I'm capable of producing shows
	But I can't reproduce!

And should you be waiting for the
director's song
Please don't hold your breath
I've fired them all!

So who wants the part?

Ensemble   (Could you do the business on the
casting couch?)

Producer   So who wants the part?

Ensemble   (Don't buy a ticket to his show from a
ticket tout!)

Producer   Which role are you going to play?

Ensemble   (Play it straight, EastEnders or play it
camp!)

Producer   If you sing and dance, why don't you come
play?

Ensemble   Producer of the show
He's producer of the show
You've all gotta go
'Cos he's producer of the show

Barman   Memory – I've such a terrible memory
I keep forgetting my–

Stage Manager   –lines !

Ensemble   Producer of the show
He's producer of the show
You've all gotta go
'Cos he's producer of the show!

5. THE HYPE MACHINE

Show producer   (*Off stage.*) And action!

(*Theme music for The Jerry Frost Show. Lights up. A paddling pool with Norma Desmond in it may be in one corner.*
David Frost-Springer *walks on with microphone into the audience.*)

Frost-Springer   Hello. Good evening and welcome.
(*He is on the wrong camera – changes position.*) London: cultural capital of Europe or Japan? Tonight we discuss London's future with health minister Selwyn Froggit, and we'll be asking the question– (*Milks the pause, then moves on to the next point.*) But first, let's turn to someone whose face you'll all come to recognise – a musical genius in the making, a purloiner of Puccini and a veritable master of the opera – will you please give a warm welcome to Sir Andrew Llob Wedders!

(*Enter **Andy** & **Tim**.*)

Tim   And me. I'm here too.

Show Producer   (*Off stage.*) Keep the camera on the ugly one!

Warm-Up Man   (*Pops on at front of house and gesticulates to audience to applaud.*)

Audience   (*Applauds.*)

Frost-Springer   (*To **Tim**.*) So, Sir Andrew–

Tim   (*Looks pleased.*) Tim.

Frost-Springer   Tim. All this success must– (*Moves hand to earpiece.*)

Show producer Not him! The camp ugly one!

Frost-Springer   (*To* **Andy***.*) So, Sir Tim–

Andy   I'm a genius you know. Come to save you from mediocre theatre.

Tim   Yes.

Frost-Springer   (*Starts to say something.*)

Andy   We're teetering on the edge of theatre world domination.

Tim   We're the employers of Prince Edward.

Frost-Springer   Well I'm sure–

Andy   (*Half-rises and declaims to cameras.*) A GENIUS, I tell you!

Frost-Springer   So what's your secret?

Andy   Secrets? Secrets?! Who said anything about secrets? I employ lawyers you know!

Tim   I write most of them, don't I Andy love? I'll get an Oscar for this! Or at least a job in Disneyland.

Andy   (*Calmer.*) It's all in the hydraulics.

Frost-Springer   Indeed.

Andy   Yes. You can't write songs without hydraulics. You try it.

Tim   We've even–

Andy   I'VE even–

Tim   Andy's even got a new show written entirely with the aid of hydraulics.

Andy   Secrets of the profession and all that. *(Laughs to himself.)*

Tim   'Sunset Pump It Up!'

Frost-Springer   Pity about the swimming pool.

Andy   It'll all come out in the wash.

Frost-Springer   I was wondering, by the way . . .

Tim   Yes?

Andy   Something on your mind?

Frost-Springer   Oh, nothing important. But there's something I've always wondered. Perhaps you could tell us?

Tim   Yes?

Andy   I'm sure we're just the chappies to help.

Frost-Springer   I don't doubt you are!

Tim   Out with it old chap!

Frost-Springer   Well now that it's one of those
unique occasions that I'm confronted by a real-life
songwriting team (**Andy** & **Tim** *look proud*) who've
ALMOST made it. (**Andy** & **Tim** *crumple.*) Explain to
me this mystery that has been perplexing me for
AGES–

Tim & Andy   Yes?

Frost-Springer   How . . .

Tim & Andy   Yes?

Frost-Springer   How– You see it's ALWAYS perplexed
me!

Tim & Andy   Yes?

Frost-Springer   How– how shall I put it?

Tim & Andy   YES?

Frost-Springer   HOW do you write those
WONDERFUL songs?

Tim   Well–

Andy   –Funny you should mention it–

Tim   –But we know a song about that–

Andy   –I do!

ANY THEME WILL JOLLY WELL DO
(Duet: **Andy** & **Tim**. *Spoken rhythmically.*)

Just take a word
And then add another
(After it)
It's so very easy
Any theme will jolly well do

We take some more words
And put them all together
   (We do!)
And rhyme with whatever
Any theme will jolly well do!
(Chorus) A dash of Hammerstein
      A smattering of Cole Porter
      West Side Story, Stephen Sonder-heim,
      Fiddler On The Roof!

And then we take some notes
We mean of music
   (We do!)
And put them altogether
Any theme will jolly well do!

We make some notes go up
And others down
   (Do re me fa so la ti do!)
Till we've got a tune
Any theme will jolly well do

(Chorus) A dash of Hammerstein
      A smattering of Cole Porter
      West Side Story, Stephen Sonder-heim,
      Fiddler On The Roof!

★

And then we take some orchestration
With members of the orchestra
       (We might even let Elton play!)*
And make them play the tunes
Any theme will jolly well do

(*Chorus*)   A dash of Hammerstein
            A smattering of Cole Porter
            West Side Story, Stephen Sonder-heim,
            Fiddler On The Roof!

And last of all
You need a story
       (Yes you do)
Put it all together and what've you got?
A musical, that's what!
Any theme will jolly well do!

          Oh yes, any theme will jolly well do
             We do
          Any theme, any theme will jolly well do
             Yes you do
          Any theme, any theme will jolly well do
             Toodleloo!

Warm-Up Man   (*Pops on at front of house and gesticulates to audience to applaud.*)

Audience   (*Applauds.*)

Frost-Springer   And now a big hand for our next guest: producer, wit, drinks canteur, Nedine McSherry's Atomic Dustbine!

Audience   (*Hoots and applauds.*)

* At this point **Andy** glares at **Tim**.

*(**Ned's Atomic Sherry** walks on to thunderous applause, waves regally and sits down. In keeping with the show, **Andy** & **Tim** look mightily dumbfounded as he nods to them.)*

Ned   Hi, Robbie!

Frost-Springer   Hi. Now, members of the audience and all the viewers watching back home, Ned has something to tell the boys. *(Hands the stage to **Ned**.)* Ned.

Ned   Boys, boys, boys and girls, I'd really like to help . . . But let's face it, this rock and roll muddled up with musicals will never work. A marvellous try though . . . If you made it a bit more Gilbert & Sullivan, 'Oklahoma!', Doris Day . . . , Rock Hudson. I might be a bit more interested. Sorry to let you down. Better luck next time!

Andy   But, but!

Frost-Springer   So what are you trying to say, Ned?

Ned   I'm so sorry. It just breaks my heart – you must have all worked so hard for it. I can see that. And now, if you don't mind, I must dash. I'm afraid I'm seeing another man. About a show. Thank you so much, au revoir!

*(The customary nail-biting and hair-pulling scrap. Bouncers leap on to separate the pugilistic guests. Exit **Frost-Springer** and **Ned's Atomic Sherry**. A big 'Aaaah!' from the audience. Long, long faces from a snivelling **Andy** & a "let-me-at-'em!" **Tim**.)*

Andy   But, but!

Show producer   Roll credits, fade out . . . stay on Quasimodo. And cut! That's a wrap boys and girls! Time to go home!

(Eventually **Tim** *stirs.)*

Tim   Well, I suppose that's that. *(Silence.)*

Andy   I suppose. *(Silence.)*

Tim   That's that. *(Silence.)*

Andy   I never liked him in any case.

(Enter **Jesús** *dragging along* **The Barman**. *Both are panting.)*

Jesús   Ah, there you are – I've been looking for you everywhere. Listen to this! Here's a funny thing! By amazing coincidence, I've just found out that Cameron Dirty-Mac here *(puts arm over* **The Barman**'s *shoulder)* is no ordinary barman. He also happens to be one of the world's most phenomenally successful theatrical producers EVER in his spare time.

Andy & Tim No!

Cameron   It's true.

Andy & Tim But we never knew!

Cameron   Well, lads, you never asked.

Jesús   And Cameron here has said that he'll only too gladly put on your show all over the world and give you oodles of money for it! Isn't that right?

Cameron   What about Nedine?

Andy   Who?

Cameron   Then the show must go on!

Andy, Tim & Jesús   Hooray!

*(**Entire cast** bursts into the chorus of 'The Producer's Song' and exits.)*

END OF ACT I

ACT TWO

8. INTRO

(**Ned's Atomic Sherry** *walks in accompanied by* **Tim**.)

Tim   So you see, Ned, we've worked extremely hard and we forgive you, and would like to give you an exclusive preview right here and now this very evening. I do hope you'll enjoy the show. Sit here. A Martini for Mr Sherry!

Ned   Thank you, thank you!

Tim   Ladies and gentlemen, and – Ned! Please take your seats! We welcome you to the first EVER performance–

Andy   Well, it's selected highlights, more like. (*Stops suddenly as* **Tim** *swiftly silences him with a suitably violent action.*)

Tim   And I would just like to take this opportunity to inform you that it is with great regret that . . . For your edification, for your delectation, for your–

Andy   Mas–

Tim   (*Puts hand swiftly over* **Andy**'s *mouth.*) Exclusively for you, Ladies and Gentlemen and – Ned, a unique presentation of the premiere performance of the world's first EVER 'rock and roll opera'! (*Uproarious and* *riotous applause.)* Music by my friend and collaborator, a talent yet to be discovered, the ever-effervescent Andrew Lloyb Webber! *(Applause.)* Book and lyrics by yours modestly truly. *(Applause.)* Ladies and Gentlemen, and – Ned, you are witness to a landmark in history – you too can say, 'I was truly there! *(Black out.)* Ladies and Gentlemen, and – Ned, I give you the rock and roll musical opera – *(under his breath)* definitely get an Oscar for this one – *(aloud)* 'Jesús-Maria Christ Super-Estar!' Take it away . . . ! *(More uproarious and riotous applause!)*

Jesús-María Christ Super Estar

A Rock And Roll Opera

The Stars:

Jesús Perón
Judás Guevara
María Perón
MC Sally Bowles King Horríd

With the Support of:

An Enlightened Reporter for Time Out
A Stern Critic for The Times
A Sinking Critic for The Mirror
An Established Director of the Theatre
A Thrusting Producer of Musicals

The Songs:

1. The Critics Will Eat You Alive
2. Some People are Born Average (Drowning Not Waving)
3. Could I Love A Failure? (Fakin' It)
4. Horríd's Rap
5. Crucify Him (*including:* Never Mind The Quality... & Beat Me Whip Me)
6. Don't Cry For Me Clapham Common
7. The Final Notice (*including:* He Is The Man, Sexstar, & The Crucifixion Can-Can)

The Story So Far...

Jesús, the much-beloved wife of the tin-pot dictator of a banana republic, cherishes deep within his heart unrealised dreams of becoming an aspiring actor of musicals.

Rejection after rejection from life's hard stage have not dulled his resolve nor blunted his thirst for fame on the boards.

One day, to his amazement, he is asked to attend an audition.

Judás Guevara and María (Mags) Perón don't think this is a good idea, for both love him – in their own way, of course – and fear for his reputation.

They plead with him, but to no avail: Jesús will not be swayed.

Trial by casting couch at the seedy West End offices of Horríd (a theatrical impresario of the theatre) proves too much for our young hero, and a tragedy unfolds of Mephistoclean proportions (Berkoff eat your heart out).

Jesús, yes, our own Jesús, finds himself ultimately and ignobly despatched by the critics – before setting even one manicured, varnished, perfect toe on those limelit boards . . .

Poor, poor shattered illusions . . . it could happen to us all!

Programme for Act II from the original production

JESÚS-MARÍA CHRIST SUPER ESTAR: A ROCK AND ROLL OPERA

(DON'T DO IT!)

Jesús *is sitting opening a massive pile of letters of rejection.*

THE CRITICS WILL EAT YOU ALIVE
(Judás *is shouting at* **Jesús.)**

What is destiny? Who knows what's in store
All the stars in the sky keep their secrets
If I could only tell the future of all
There'd be no need for all our secrets

Jesús . . .
Who gave you those starstruck eyes
Who filled your head with all those lies
And told you that one day you'll be a star?
Yes life's a cabaret old chum
But there's no 'welkom' on that stage
There must be other ways for you to find your fun.

Listen Jesús I'm utterly confounded by what I hear
They're telling me that you haven't any fear
And you've been saying you're gonna be a star
They've told you that you've got the part
If the audition works out right
And they'll have your name in bright lights one day

★

There'll come a time of agents with fat Havana Cigars
Glitzy starlets with underwired bras
Waving contracts and much, much worse right in
your face
The rags will want to know whose thongs you wear
Fairweather friends will want to share
Your holidays in San Moritz . . .
But how can you be the Son of God?
You owe nothing to that old mean sod
He hasn't been seen since he left your mum in the club
So you can't really be the new Messiah–
You were never one of life's great triers
You'd be much better off coming home with me!

Jesús when are you gonna admit defeat?
Showbiz! Ain't it time to stand on your feet
'Cos we still respect you from your head down to
your toes
The offer ain't the part of your lifetime
But a loaded gun against your head
Much better to hold your breath in bed.

(Interlude.)

I'm not jealous, no please don't get me wrong
And please don't think I'm coming on far too strong
But let's face it Jeez you ain't no James Dean.

You're a man and no Messiah
One day they'll cast you in the fire
On the first night the critics will eat you
Alive
Oh yes they'll eat
You
Alive!

Jesús　　　*(Opening final letter.)* I've got my first
audition, yes!

María　　　Don't do it – they'll crucify you!

Judás　　　The stage is no place for a talent like yours!

Jesús　　　No it's my destiny. I'm going to show them
what I've got. I've GOT to show them what I've got.

SOME PEOPLE ARE BORN AVERAGE
(DROWNING NOT WAVING)

(**María Magdalena** *sings of her concern for* **Jesús** *and how he
can do whatever he wants and how he shouldn't take any notice of*
Judás *who's just jealous and has read too many Joe Orton biogs*)

Mary　　　Some people are born bubbles
　　　　　　That burst in the warm sunlight
　　　　　　While others have silver spoons
　　　　　　Rammed up their bums
　　　　　　But don't worry if
　　　　　　You have no personality
　　　　　　Don't try to be more
　　　　　　Than what you are–

　　　　　　　　　You're a star,
　　　　　　　　　You're a star,
　　　　　　　　　You're star,
　　　　　　　　　You're a star,
　　　　　　　　　Boy, tonight!

Mary & Jesús　　　Some people have talent
　　　　　　　　Others lots of money
　　　　　　　　But don't let yourself worry
　　　　　　　　If you have none

Because someone has to be normal
Average and dumb
And I think it could be
You tonight

You're a star,
You're a star,
You're star,
You're a star,
Boy, tonight!

Mary & Jesús Some people are born bubbles
That burst in the warm sunlight
While others have silver spoons
Rammed up their bums
Mary, Jesús & Judás But don't worry if
You have no personality
Don't try to be more
Than what you are

You're a star,
You're a star,
You're star,
You're a star,
Boy, tonight!
You're a star,

You're a star,
You're star,
Boy, tonight!

(Fade out) Average Joe go with the flow
Be someone boring tonight
Some people are born boring
Some people are born boring . . .

Judás   But Jesús, please don't go! I care for you. I'm concerned for you. They'll do nasty things to you. I love you!

Jesús   I love you too, Judás – as a friend. I hear the call – can't you understand that?

COULD I LOVE A SAILOR?
(**Judás** *sings of his unrequited love for* **Jesús**.)

I think I really love him
He's the best, always laughing
He's my man, he is the man
And I want him so, let the world know
Our love dare not speak its name

I could nip down to a disco,
The YMCA or a sauna
And find a man, just any man
And I've had so many men before
In many different ways
              He's just one more hole

              Should I stand out proud
              Should I shriek and shout
              Should I party loud
              Tell the world I'm out
              I never dreamed I'd come like this
              Now all I feel is doubt . . .

Don't you think it's rather funny
I should be in this position
I'm the one who's always been
In calm control, a dominant pole
Taking every hole
              He intrigues me so

★

Should I stand out proud
Should I shriek and shout
Should I party loud
Tell the world I'm out
I never dreamed I'd come like this
So what's that about then?

But if he says he wants my cherry
What to do – should I play hard to get?
Would I cope, or sit and mope
Cry my tears, submit to fears
Curse the day I met him so?
He intrigues me so
I desire him so
I lust after him so . . .

(**Jesús** *meanwhile has arrived at the audition. A sign says
'Casting Couch tonite' – the word 'couch' is crossed out.*)

Horrid: Next! (**Jesús** *nervously comes on.*) Name?

Jesús: Jesús Christ, ahem, Super Estar.

Horrid: Well, okay, 'Super', what've you got for us?

Jesús: I've come about the part for the show.

Horrid: Well I know THAT! What've you GOT?
Show us some tricks! Flaunt your stuff, baby!

Jesús: (*Faintly.*) My . . . STUFF?

Horrid: Yeah, your stuff! This is a show you're
auditioning for. You gotta have stuff to flaunt, tricks to
spin, talents (*leers*) to REVEAL!

Jesús: Talents?

Horrid: You got talents?

Jesús: Yes, but–

Horrid: So tell me, Jesús, have you ever seen a grown man in the nude?

Jesús: I . . . I . . .

Horrid: Did you ever go into the showers after a really hot, sweaty football game with the rest of the BOYS?

Jesús: Yes, I suppose so, but, football . . . ? I've come to perform!

Horrid: Haven't we all? Did you ever wonder if you could know your REAL self?

Jesús: My–? *(Slumps into a pool of tears.)*

Horrid: *(Drawls.)* Oh dear!

HORRÍD'S RAP
(**Horríd** *raps this as a Leading Critic.*)

Horríd	**Tell me Jesús**
Ensemble	**(Yeah!)**
Horríd	**Are you truly the Great Messiah?**
Ensemble	**(Yes!)**
Horríd	**Truly the Son of God**
	Who's come to drag us from the mire?
Ensemble	**(Hallelujah!)**
Horríd	**When I'm in your presence, dude**

I find I don't know where to turn
The wonder boy is here, my friends,
He even walks on sperm

Will there come a time, aye,
Of flash mobile phones
(Do I hear you say . . . ?)

Ensemble   (Yeah!)
Horríd   Interest-free gold indexed loans
Good mortgage rates on your homes

I've a favour to ask
It'll be no hard task
Come on you thespian star

If you are the Christ, Trinity
With God and the Holy Dove
You must have skills vested
In you by the powers above
So even though you're schizo,
Your personality of three
We can sit here on my casting couch
And see what you'll do for me

Why don't you cut right in half
My MASSIVE bank overdraft
And you know how a bad thirst kills
Turn my water into Holsten Pils

I've a favour to ask
It'll be no hard task
Come on you thespian star

Interlude during which **Jesús** *pleads:* 'But I've come to save you all from mediocre theatre! Why don't you listen to me?'

Horríd	Tell me Jesús
Ensemble	(Yeah!)
Horríd	Are you truly the Great Messiah?
Ensemble	(Yes!)
	Cause the blind to see,
	Make cripples walk,
	Turn my nipples hard,
	INSPIRED?
Ensemble	(Hallelujah!)
Horríd	When I'm in your presence, dude,
	I find I don't know where to turn
	The wonder boy is here, my friends,
	He even walks on sperm

★

	I find your attitude so damn
	Mapplethorpe
Ensemble	(Yeah!)
Horríd	Don't you know that talent talks
Ensemble	(Genuflect genuflect!)
Horríd	Come Jeez give me Madonna's body
Ensemble	(Madonna?)
Ensemble	(Her body?!)
Horríd	*(Spoken.)* You don't know what it's like to be

trapped in a man's body!

Ensemble	(Aaargh!)

Horríd	*(Raps slowly while stripping.)*
	Well look I've a favour to ask
	It'll be no hard task
	Come on you thespian star–

Jesús   Stop! I don't have to prove ANYTHING!! I
will be a star. I AM a star!

Horríd & Ensemble   Oh dear!

Pilates   Well then, we're going to have you.

Horríd   Yes. In more ways than one.

THE CRITICS' SONG
(Jesús *and* Critics 1 & 2, Director, Producer.)

Critic 1   I'm a writer for 'The Mirror'
Critic 2   I'm a critic for 'The Times'
Critic 1   We write reviews
Critic 2   We have our views

Director   I'm a director of the theatre
Producer   I'm a producer of musicals
Director   We have our views
Producer   We cause reviews

Jesús   Don't waste your time scribbling your words
     Nothing can convey the magic of me
     I'm a prodigy you see – a true shining star
     You have to just experience the quality

     Never mind the quality
     Just come and feel the width
     It's the magic of a true star
     You will know it when you see it
     Hit you in the face

All   Jesús-María Christ Super Estar

Critic 1   I'm a writer for 'The Mirror'
Critic 2   I'm a critic for 'The Times'
Critic 1   We write reviews
Critic 2   We have our views

Director	I'm a director of the theatre
Producer	I'm a producer of musicals
Director	We have our views
Producer	We cause reviews

Jesús
Never mind the quality
Just come and feel the width
It's the magic of a true star
You will know it when you see it
Hit you in the face

All
Jesús-María Christ Super Estar
Jesús-María Christ Super Estar!

Jesús *(Speaks.)* I want to be on the stage!–

(Sings.) Beat me whip me castigate me
Flay me slay me cast-a-rate me
You won't divert me you won't deflect me
From my destiny!

BEAT ME, WHIP ME
(Jesús & Ensemble.)

Beat me, spank me, whip me, rip my flesh to shreds
Flagellate me till I'm black and red
Hit me I'm all fired
Don't you dare get tired
Lash me, bash me and thrash me hard.

Beat me, spank me, whip me, rip my flesh to shreds
Flagellate me till I'm black and red
Hit me, I'm all fired
Don't you dare get tired
Lash me, bash me and thrash me hard.

★

(Faster.)
Beat me, spank me, whip me, rip my flesh to shreds
Flagellate me till I'm black and red
Hit me, I'm all fired
Don't you dare get tired
Lash me, bash me and thrash me hard.

(Slow, gasping.)
Beat me, spank me, whip me, rip my flesh to shreds
Flagellate me till I'm black and red
Hit me, I'm all fired
Don't you dare get tired
Lash me, bash me and thrash me hard.

(Slow oom pah pah.)
Beat me, spank me, whip me, rip my flesh to shreds
Flagellate me till I'm black and red
Hit me, I'm all fired
Don't you dare get tired
Lash me, bash me and thrash me hard.

(Al tempo.)
Beat me, spank me, whip me, rip my flesh to shreds
Flagellate me till I'm black and red
Hit me, I'm all fired
Don't you dare get tired
Lash me, bash me and thrash me hard.

(All collapse in a heaving heap.)

Horrid   Beat you?

Critic 1   Castrate you?

Critic 2   Oh no, we have special clubs for that sort of thing!

Horríd   Yes! I've got a card.

Jesús   I have come to save you all from mediocre theatre!

Horríd   Oh no we don't want any of that.

Critic 1   Star quality? Isn't that astronomy or something?

Critic 2   I've wiped my arse with less. I think.

Horríd   Crucify him?

All   Crucify him.

(In background plays Pacheval's Canon on organ.)

Reporter   Crucifixion?

Jesús   Yes.

Reporter   Good, good. I'm a junior reporter and I'll just take your details. Just a few personal details so we know how to make it as painful as possible . . .

Jesús   Oh.

Reporter   Good. So let's start shall we? We'll start off with the simple ones: Surname?

Jesús   Christ

Reporter   Jewish name?

Jesús   Jesús.

Reporter	Middle name?
Jesús	H.
Reporter	Father?
Jesús	God.
Reporter	How are you spelling that?
Jesús	G.O.D.
Reporter	'G-od.' Mother?
Jesús	Mary.
Reporter	Surname?
Jesús	Blessed Virgin.
Reporter	Religion? Jewish?
Jesús	Only on my mother's side.
Reporter	'Only on mother's side.' Birth?
Jesús	Immaculate.
Reporter	No I mean DATE of birth.
Jesús	Oh – 25, 12, zero.
Reporter	Place of birth?
Jesús	Manger?

Reporter	Is that Manger in Essex or in Kent?
Jesús	Kent.
Reporter	Occupation?
Jesús	Carpent– no, SUPER ESTAR!
Reporter	'Super Estar.' All right, then. Thank you very much for your patience. I think it's now . . .

Reporter & Ensemble CRUCIFIXION TIME!

(**Jesús** *is crucified on cross made of newspaper reviews and theatre posters.*)

Jesús   No, no, please don't. That hurts! Ow!

DON'T CRY FOR ME CLAPHAM JUNCTION
(**Jesús** *sings from the cross with a country & western twang.*)

Clapham Junction
Clapham Junction . . .

It makes me queasy, you'll think it strange
When I try to explain my range
Yes I'm a singer you see an artiste of the stage
You won't believe me–
All that you see is a boy you once knew
Crucified here on the stage
The critics have worked their foul brew.

I used to practise on platform four
Yes I'm a singer but I can do more
I can dance, do accents and mime on the side

So I chose Clapham
Busking around the ticket booking hall
Singing arias and busting my balls
But made no impression at all

> Don't die on me
> Clapham Junction
> Who knows what might have been
> All through life's foreplay, our sad persistence
> Will you please hang on in there
> While I go the distance?

I tried for fortune, oh I tried for fame
I never got them, oh what a shame
Yes I'm an artiste you see, a star of the stage
I need my public
The audience I love and who'll always adore me
I'll never forget you even after you've gone
I KNOW you'll never forget me

> Don't die on me–
> Clapham Junction
> Mmm . . .

> Don't die on me
> Clapham Junction
> The truth is we'll meet again
> All through life's foreplay, our sad persistence
> Will you please hang on in there
> While I go the distance?

(Spoken most sincerely.)
Oh I've gushed too much!
There ain't nuthin' more
That comes to mind
That I can tell you, folks.

But all you gotta do
Is look deep in your heart,
And look me in the eye,
And I know
That you know
That every word is true . . .

(Mutters in a choked voice.) Now y'all drive home carefully now . . . ! *(Puts his head down to die.)*

Judas   Poor Jesús. Condemned before he even started. Slated before he even set foot on the stage. Hounded by the press, panned by the critics, shunned by the public. Every back was turned on him, not a soul lent a favourable review! Not a soul . . . !

María   A talent strangled at birth. Poor Jesús.

Judás   He set his ideals too high.

María   He flew too high and got burned.

Judás   He failed as a thespian.

María   He never reached his star . . .

Judás   Poor, poor shattered illusions . . . It could happen to us all.

THE FINAL NOTICE
(*including:* HE IS THE MAN, SUPER ESTAR & THE CRUCIFIXION CAN CAN)
(**Judás** *&* **Cast** *sing to* **Jesús** *as he hangs from the cross of reviews.)*

Judás   Can't you see you've only got yourself
                                    now to blame?

> For why you never climbed that ladder of
> fame?
> Maybe martyrdom is the only way to get
> a name
> But the only thing that springs to mind is
> 'Oh what a shame!'

Ensemble

> Listen to what the man says
> Listen to what the man says
> (Oh yeah)
> Listen to what the man says
> (YEAH!) He is the man!

Judás

> Don't you look at me with those glistening
> eyes
> It wasn't me who filled you up with those
> mad lies
> I'd blame your folks – they said that
> you'd be a star
> Now I bet you're hanging wondering
> Where the holy fuck you are!

Ensemble

> Listen to what the man says
> Listen to what the man says
> (Oh yeah)
> Listen to what the man says
> (YEAH!) He is the man!

Judás

> Jesús now it's time for you to admit defeat
> Showbiz failed you, you've been knocked
> off your feet
> Your career's gone wrong and now babe
> you'll never know
> Now you're hanging there wondering
> where the holy fuck to go!

★

Ensemble

Listen to what the man says
Listen to what the man says
(Oh yeah)
Listen to what the man says
(YEAH!) He is the man!

Judás

(Speaks over the next two verses.)
Oh my God he's rising
Oh my
He's rising
I can't believe it
Cover your eyes
It's enormous!
He's coming!

Ensemble

Listen to what the man says
Listen to what the man says
(Oh yeah)
Listen to what the man says
(YEAH!) He is the man!

Listen to what the man says
Listen to what the man says
(Oh yeah)
Listen to what the man says
(YEAH!) He is the man!

Jesús Christ one day you'll be a star
All you gotta do is believe in who you are
Jesús Christ one day you'll be a star
All you gotta do is believe in who you are
Jesús Christ one day you'll be a star
All you gotta do is believe in who you are!

(A cappella.) Jesús Christ one day you'll be a star
All you gotta do is believe in who you are

Jesús Christ one day you'll be a star
All you gotta do is believe in who you are
Jesús Christ one day you'll be a star
All you gotta do is believe in who you are!

(Music. Faster.)

Jesús Christ one day you'll be a star
All you gotta do is believe in who you are
Jesús Christ one day you'll be a star
All you gotta do is believe in who you are
Jesús Christ one day you'll be a star
All you gotta do is believe in who you
are . . .

Judás & Ensemble Jonah And His Amazing
Technicolor Yawn
Jesús-María Christ Super Estar
Heaves, Eeek! Eat Her, Bum and
Prance
Prats, Beeching Express, Daisy
Jerks It Off*
Wreck 'Em, Tank 'Em For The
Opera, Aspic Offal
Sunset Bollockfart, Widdle Down
The Wind
The Crying Shame, Bum Boy
Screams . . .

*(**Jesús** rises from the crucifix and they all do a slow can-can –
'The Crufixion Can-Can' – to a thunderous finale.)*

T H E   E N D

---

* For the more earnest trainspotters only: not strictly part of the Llob-Wedder pantheon.

OTHER BOOKS FROM DESERT♥HEARTS

The Vibrators:
20 Years of Pure Mania
Ian 'Knox' M. Carnochan

Knox – lead singer and principal songwriter
with one of the original punk bands of the
1970s the VIBRATORS – covers the band's
history from its original inception in 1976, all
the way through to 1997. With plenty of
photos and illustration, this is a must for
anyone with the slightest interest in the
band.

ISBN 1 898948 10 0 £8.99 ring-bound

I Saw Satan on the
Northern Line:
Love Songs from the
Underground
Nick Awde

A CD-sized collection of satirical verse
on life, love and London.

ISBN 1 898948 00 3 £5.99 paperback

Desert♥Hearts, PO Box 2131, London W1A 5SU, England
desertheartsuk@hotmail.com